# Discover Writing Discover Korea 9

# [여는 말]

한국에는 수준 높은 좋은 영어 교재들이 많이 있습니다. 그러나 이들 중 대부분의 책들은 한국 학생들의 삶과 문화에 진정으로 연결되어 있지 않고, 외국 문화와 맥락으로 가득 차 있습니다. 학생들이 교재의 내용에 공감하지 못해 영어에 대한 관심을 잃는 것을 보며 이러한 의문들이 들기 시작했습니다. "만약 한국 문화를 중심으로 한 교제가 있다면 어떨까?", "만약 교재가 학생들의 일상 생활과 더 밀접하게 연결되어 있다면 어떨까?".

이렇게 시작된 "만약"은 "나도 어쩌면 작은 변화를 가져올 수 있다."는 생각의 씨앗이 되었습니다. 모든 것을 바꿀 방법은 없을지도 모르지만, 제가 시작점이 되어 한국 학생들을 위한, 한국 문화를 반영한 영어 학습 자료, 그리고 학생들에게 친숙하고 위로가 되는 학습자료를 제공하고 싶었습니다.

**Discover Writing Discover Korea** 시리즈는 **총 5 권**으로 구성되어 있습니다. 이 시리즈는 제목에서도 선명하게 보이듯이 영어 글쓰기를 위한 책입니다. 이 5 권의 책시리즈들은 **각 장르별 영어 글쓰기 스킬을 제공**하면서 동시에 **다른 책에서 다루지 않는 문법의 일면들을 제공**하고 있습니다. 이 책을 통해 또한 **학생들은 자기평가가 가능**합니다. 보통의 교실환경에서 학생들은 주로 평가를 받는 입장입니다. 학생들은 점수에만 매인 채 평가의 의미와 결과의 이유는 잘 알지 못합니다. 이 책에서는 학습자가 평가의 주체가 되어 봄으로서 새로운 시각으로 본인의 글을 볼 수 있는 기회를 제공합니다. 학습자들은 **친숙한 한국문화를** 밑바탕으로 낯선 컨텐츠에 방해받지 않고 쓰기학습이라는 **본연의 목적에 충실**할 수 있도록 설계되었습니다.

저는 **진정한 영어 글쓰기를 위한 쓰기교육**을 학생들이 이 책과 함께 이루어 나가길 소망합니다. 학생들이 이 책에 빠져들며 영어 글쓰기 실력을 향상시키고 진정한 학습의 기쁨을 맛볼 수 있기를 진심으로 바랍니다.

이 책이 만들어지기까지 항상 용기를 주었던 나의 가족들, 학교 동기 선생님들, 교수님들, 친구들 그리고 나의 학생들과 학부형님 모두에게 감사 인사를 드리고 싶습니다.

나의 고민을 함께해주며 같이 울고 웃어준 나의 남편, 전화한통도 조심스러웠던 양가 부모님과 표지 제작에 많은 도움을 준 내 동생, 항상 용기를 주시고 나의 가치를 인정해 주셨던 성희선생님, 지선선생님, 그리고 소중한 오랜 인연 해정님, 멋진 코믹을 사용할 수 있게 기회를 열어 주신 PIXTON, 지금의 책이 있을 수 있게 열정적인 조언을 주셨던 정은영 교수님과 박혜옥 교수님, 그리고 누구보다 나의 발전에 불을 지피고 영감을 주며 지켜봐 주신 Chris 교수님께 special thanks 를 드리고 싶습니다.

**[Prologue]**

In Korea, there are many high-quality English textbooks available. However, most of these books are not genuinely connected to the lives and culture of Korean students; they are filled with foreign contexts and cultures. It saddened me to see students unable to relate to the content of these textbooks, causing them to lose interest in learning English. This raised questions in my mind: "What if there were materials centered around Korean culture?" "What if textbooks were closely linked to students' daily lives?"

These "what ifs" planted the seed of the thought, "Perhaps I can make a small change." While I may not be able to change everything, I wanted to be the starting point for providing English learning materials that reflect Korean culture and are familiar and comforting to students.

**The "Discover Writing Discover Korea" series is comprised of a total of 10 volumes.** As clearly indicated by its title, this series is a book for English writing. These ten volumes offer English **writing skills specific to various genres while also providing aspects of grammar not covered in other books.** Through this series, **students can also conduct self-evaluation**. In typical classroom environments, students are usually on the receiving end of evaluations. They are often bound to scores, not fully understanding the meaning of the evaluations or the reasons behind their results. This book gives learners the opportunity to become the evaluators themselves, allowing them to see their writing from a new perspective. The series is designed so that learners can remain true to the fundamental goal of writing education without being hindered by unfamiliar content, **based on the familiar backdrop of Korean culture.**

I hope that students embark on a journey of true English writing education with these books. I sincerely wish for them to immerse themselves in these books, improve their English writing skills, and experience the true joy of learning.

I would like to express my gratitude to my family, schoolmates, teachers, friends, and all my students and fellow educators who have always supported me in the creation of this book.

To my husband, who shared my concerns and laughed and cried with me, to my cautious parents who were always just a phone call away, to my younger sister who provided invaluable assistance in designing the cover, to Seonghee and Jisun, who always encouraged me and recognized my worth; to my precious long-time friend, Hae-jung; to PIXTON for opening the opportunity to use amazing comics, to Professor Eun-young Jeong and Professor Hye-ok Park, who provided passionate advice and most importantly, to Professor Chris Douloff, who has been a source of inspiration, guidance, and unwavering support in my personal growth—special thanks to you all.

# ORGANIZATION OF THE BOOK

## 01 Drawing the Big Picture
Lesson Map
Module Objective

## 02 Components of a Lesson
Keywords
Getting Ready to Write
Pen-to-paper Ideas
Writing Tips
Common Saying
Grammar

## 03 Writing and Self-assessment
Write with Your Teacher
Summative Assessment
Student Survey Questionnaire

## 04 The Section for Teachers
formative Assessment
Rubric for the Module
Teacher's Diaries
Guide by Growth

# INTRODUCTION OF TLC, GENRE WRITING, AND PROCESS WRITING

The teaching-learning cycle, genre writing, and process writing are three effective methods that interrelate and complement each other in fostering students' writing skills.

## 1. Teaching-Learning Cycle (TLC)

The Teaching-Learning Cycle is a systematic approach to teaching that involves four stages: **building the field** (contextualizing and building background knowledge), **modeling** (showcasing examples), **joint construction** (collaborative writing), and **independent construction** (students write on their own).

**Relation to Other Methods:** TLC acts as a framework where genre writing and process writing can be incorporated. For example, while modeling, you can introduce different genres and engage students in the process of writing stages.

**Application:** Start by engaging students with images or discussions to build context (**Building the Field**). Then, provide a well-structured example text (**Modelling**), followed by collaborative writing (**Joint Construction**). Finally, allow students to write independently.

## 2. Genre Writing

Genre writing focuses on teaching students about different text types or genres such as narratives, reports, or persuasive texts, and **the language features and structures commonly used** in each.

**Relation to Other Methods**: Within the TLC, different genres can be modeled and practiced. Process writing can be applied within a specific genre to go through the drafting, revising, and editing stages.

**Application**: Choose a **genre** and **model a text**, discussing its **specific language features** and **structures**. Then, **guide** students to write their own texts following the conventions of the chosen genre.

## 3. Process Writing

Process writing emphasizes the steps or processes in writing such as planning, drafting, revising, editing, and publishing.

**Relation to Other Methods:** It can be embedded within the TLC during the independent construction phase and can be utilized across different genres.

**Application**: Guide students through each stage, from brainstorming ideas (**Planning**), writing a first draft (**Drafting**), getting and giving feedback (**Revising**), correcting errors (**Editing**), to finally publishing their work.

**The integration of these three methods** offers a **comprehensive, structured, and student-centered approach to teaching writing**, which supports students in becoming autonomous, reflective, and proficient writers.

# TABLE OF CONTENTS

# Lesson Map

| Module 9: Blog Writing | | | | | | |
|---|---|---|---|---|---|---|
| **Get Ready to Write** | | | | **Write** | | **Revise & Edit** |
| Keywords | Model Texts | Pen-to-paper Ideas & Writing Tips | Grammar | Write with your Teacher | Write by Yourself | Editing |
| Reach out, opportunity, exchange, look for, patient, insight, advanced, navigate, immerse, enthusiasm. | **I'm Looking for a Unique and Exciting Opportunity: A Language Exchange Partner!** | • understanding and apply the format of blog structures.<br><br>• build basic analytical skills to share the student writer's insightful opinions clearly.<br><br>• apply a sense of connection with the audience, making the writing relatable and interesting.<br><br>• Common Saying: *I'm eager to improve my skills.* | • How to use a colon<br><br>• how to use a semi-colon | • completing the unfinished part of a blog text | • challenge: write an advertisement under the given prompts | • check a colon and semi-colon |

**Example Lesson Plans: Module 1** [8 classes, 6 hours]

| Module objectives | *By the end of* **Module 1**, *a student will be better able to* |
|---|---|
| ⭐ 2 | **O1.** compose a self-introduction using simple, short sentences, and a first-person perspective considering the readership and purpose of the text. **O2.** understand language in chunks and fixed expressions **O3.** share personal information safely and appropriately, and use the appropriate tone. **O4.** apply simple vocabulary and present tense **O5.** understand the rules of the S-V agreement and apply them in writing. |
| **Legend** | TLC = Teaching learning cycle |
| **Class 1** | TLC stage: *Modelling* |
| **Major Stages** | **1.** Explain module objectives to S |
| | **2. "Task A"** (1–5): Have S read questions and discuss. |
| | **3. "KEYWORDS":** Have S check the target words and elicit their meaning. Help S pronounce words correctly. If needed, use **MORE EXERCISE FOR KEYWORDS** |
| | **4. "Model Text":** Have S read the given cartoon and understand the context. Give S a "Model Text" and encourage S to notice the target words in the text. Have S understand the content of the text using concept-checking questions (CCQ). |
| **HW** | **"HOMEWORK DAY 1"** |
| **Class 2** | TLC stage: *Modelling* |
| **Major Stages** | 1. 1. **"HOMEWORK DAY 1"**: to check + **"KEYWORDS"**: to review + **"Model Text"**: to review |
| | **"WRITING STRATEGIES—"Writing Process"**: Have S read and discuss. |
| | 1. **"DEEP DIVE":** Have S analyze **"Model Text"**. Have S consider the structure. S applies to **"DEEP DIVE A & B"**. If a learner doesn't have a partner, the teacher fills that role as a guide. Don't forget that the teacher's role is not only to teach but also to observe, and guide |
| **HW** | **"HOMEWORK DAY 2"** |
| **Class 3** | TLC stage: *Modelling* |

| | |
|---|---|
| **Major Stages** | 1. **"HOMEWORK DAY 2"**: to check + **"KEYWORDS"**: to review + **"Model Text"**: to review |
| | 2. **KEY ELEMENT & TIPS**—"**Self-introduction Etiquette"(Tip 1–6):** to check S understands tips for writing self-introduction. Have S complete **"EXERCISE 1, 2"**, **"HANDS-ON ACTIVITIES A, B"**, and **"DEEP DIVE A, B"**. |
| | 3. **"SUMMARY"**: to review a letter-writing process |
| **HW** | **"HOMEWORK DAY 3"** |
| **Class 4** | TLC stage: *Modelling* |
| **Major Stages** | 1. **"HOMEWORK DAY 3"**: to check + **"KEYWORDS"**: to review + **"Model Text"**: to review + **"Self-introduction Etiquette"(Tip1-6)**: to review |
| | 2. **KEY ELEMENT & TIPS** —**Fixed Expression**: Have S read examples and elicit the expression's meaning. Have S solve "EXERCISE 3–5". |
| | 3. "**DEEP DIVE**": Have S read **"Model Text"** and analyze the fixed expression in the text. |
| **HW** | **"HOMEWORK DAY 3"** |
| **Class 5** | TLC stage: *Modelling* |
| **Major Stages** | 1. **"GRAMMAR 1"**: Have S think about when to use the present tense. Have S read **"GRAMMAR 1"** and provide some time to notice the function of the present tense. Have S solve **"EXERCISE 6"**. Conduct **CCQ.** |
| | 2. **"DEEP DIVE A-D"**: Have S read "Model Text" and analyze. |
| | 3. **"HANDS-ON ACTIVITIES A, B:** Have S solve. |
| **HW** | **"HOMEWORK DAY 5"** |
| **Class 6** | TLC stage: *Modelling* |
| **Major Stages** | 1. **"HOMEWORK DAY 5"**: to check + **"KEYWORDS"**: to review + **"Model Text"**: to review + **Self-introduction Etiquette (Tip1-6)** to review + **"Fixed Expression"**: to review + **"GRAMMAR 1"**: to review |
| | 2. "**GRAMMAR 2-1**": Have S think about the rule of present Be-verb. Have S read **"GRAMMAR 2-1"**. Have S solve **"EXERCISE 7"**. **Conduct CCQ.** |
| | 2. "**GRAMMAR 2-2**": Have S think about the rule of present Action-verb. Have S read **"GRAMMAR 2-2"**. Have S solve **"EXERCISE 8"**. **Conduct CCQ.** |

| | |
|---|---|
| | 3. "**HANDS-ON ACTIVITIES**": S makes sentences in "HANDS-ON ACTIVITIES A, B". |
| **HW** | "**HOMEWORK DAY 6**" |
| **Class 7** | TLC stage: *joint construction1 –2* |
| **Major Stages** | 1. "**HOMEWORK DAY 6**": to check + "**KEYWORDS**": to review + "**Model Text**": to review + **Self-introduction Etiquette (Tip1-6)** to review + "**Fixed Expression**": to review + "**GRAMMAR 1**": to review "**GRAMMAR 1**": to review +"**GRAMMAR 2-1, 2-2**": to review |
| | 2. "**WRITE WITH YOUR TEACHER 1**": Have S understand the purpose of the task. Guide S to complete the unfinished text. Demonstrate S how to revise and edit using the checklist. |
| | 3. "**WRITE WITH YOUR TEACHER 2**": Have S understand the task's purpose and demonstrate the process writing procedure. Complete the task with S. |
| **HW** | "**HOMEWORK DAY 7**" |
| **Class 8** | TLC stage: *Independent construction* |
| **Major Stages** | 1. "**HOMEWORK DAY 7**": to check + "**KEYWORDS**": to review + "**Model Text**": to review + **Self-introduction Etiquette (Tip1-6)** to review + "**Fixed Expression**": to review + "**GRAMMAR 1**": to review "**GRAMMAR 1**": to review +"**GRAMMAR 2-1, 2-2**": to review + "**WRITE WITH YOUR TEACHER 2**": to review the procedure of process writing |
| | 2. "**INDEPENDENT WRITING**": Have S understand the purpose of the task. Have S look through and complete the task. |

**I'M LOOKING FOR A UNIQUE AND EXCITING OPPORTUNITY: A LANGUAGE EXCHANGE PARTNER!**

## MODULE OBJECTIVES

In this module, you will learn how to

- organize the text in a blog structure
- analyze the elements of each part
- explain the reason and purpose of the advertisement
- understand the procedures of pre-writing, drafting, revising, and editing.

**A.** Answer the questions. Discuss with your partner.
1. Have you read any advertisements online? What kind of was it?
2. Who wrote it?
3. What did the writer want to say in the advertisement?
4. Are Korean online advertisements and English ones similar or different?

## KEYWORDS

Match the words with pictures. Check the meanings and pronunciation with your teacher.

Learning about Korean history can give you deep _____ into the country's culture.    ▪

▪ reach out

Always _____ to your teacher if you don't understand the lesson.    ▪

▪ look for

To understand Hangeul better, you need to _____ yourself in daily practice.    ▪

▪ opportunity

In the exchange program, you will have the _____ to learn about Korean culture.    ▪

▪ exchange

South Korea's _____ transportation system makes traveling around the country quick and easy.    ▪

▪ patient

It's important to be _____ when learning a new language.    ▪

▪ advanced

▪

▪ insight

▪

▪ immerse

▪

▪ navigate

▪

▪ enthusiasm for

# MORE EXERCISE FOR KEYWORDS

**Exercise 1**. Check the meaning of each word above again. Put them with the word that takes the same role in each box together. Work with your partner. Follow an example.

| e.g., apple, bus, cat… | e.g., pretty, soft, big… | e.g., eat, have, run… |
|---|---|---|
|  |  |  |

**Exercise 2**. Check the pronunciation and stress of each word. Work with your partner. Follow an example.

●
op▪por▪tun▪ity

●
im▪merse

●
en▪thu▪si▪asm

●
navi▪gate

★ 4

**Exercise 3**. Look up the words again. Can you guess what story is in the text? Discuss with your partner.

# MORE EXERCISE FOR KEYWORDS

**Exercise 4**. Fill in the gap with the words below.

| reach out, opportunity, exchange, look for, patient, insight, advanced, navigate, immerse, enthusiasm |
| --- |

1. This summer camp is a great _____ for kids to learn about nature.

2. The new game app is quite _____, with lots of detailed features.

3. Diving into a good book can _____ you in a whole new world.

4. In the foreign language class, students often _____ cultural information with their classmates.

5. Her _____ for learning Korean made her study every day.

6. It can be tricky to _____ through the city without a map.

7. The _____ technology in smartphones makes our lives easier.

8. After being sick for a week, Mark had to _____ on all the lessons he missed.

9. The teacher's _____ for teaching history makes the class more interesting.

10. To learn French, you must _____ yourself in the language and culture.

11. Reading books gives you deeper _____ into different cultures and ideas.

12. It's important to _____ to friends who may be feeling sad or alone.

13. I always _____ my keys in the morning before leaving for school.

14. Our trip to the science museum was an exciting _____ to learn about space.

15. When you don't understand a lesson, it's a good idea to _____ to your teacher for help.

## MODULE 9   WHAT SHALL I DO TO FIND A LANGUAGE EXCHANGE PARTNER?

Sally wants to practice Korean more. Now, she is looking for the way of doing it with her uncle Oliver.

Comic made at Pixton.com

## Model Text

**Title**

: It is like the name of your story or article. It tells the reader what your writing is about. Here, the title suggests that the writer wants to find someone to learn languages with.

### Language Exchange Opportunity: Let's Learn Together!

Comic made at Pixton.com

**Introduction**

: This is the beginning of your writing. You introduce yourself and tell the reader what you are going to talk about. In this case, the writer introduces herself, tells us her age and where she's from, and explains that she wants to find a language exchange partner.

.

Hello everyone! My name is A-young and I'm a 14-year-old student from South Korea. I'm reaching out to all of you through this blog because I'm looking for a unique and exciting opportunity: a language exchange partner!

I have been studying English for a few years now and I'm eager to improve my skills. However, I believe the best way to learn a language is by speaking with native speakers. That's why I'm looking for a girl around my age, 14 to 15 years old, who is interested in learning Korean and can help me with my English.

Here's what I'm hoping to find in a language exchange partner:
- A native English speaker who is interested in learning Korean.
- Someone around 14-15 years old, so we can have more in common.
- A friendly and patient person, as we both are learning.

In return, I promise to:
- Help you with your Korean language skills, from basics to more advanced topics.
- Share insights about Korean culture, food, and traditions.
- Be a patient and understanding partner as we navigate learning together.

**Reasons**
: In this part, this writer explains why she thinks a language exchange is a good idea. It's like giving reasons or explaining why something is important. She talks about the benefits of learning a language by talking with someone who speaks it naturally.

Language exchange is a great way to learn because it allows us to immerse ourselves in another language and culture. We can learn how people actually talk in everyday life, not just the words we see in textbooks. Plus, it's a fun way to make a new friend from a different part of the world!

**Main body**

**Part 1:**
**Background and Objective**

: This section explains the writer's background in learning English and her objective. It outlines her reasoning for wanting a language exchange partner and specifies the criteria for her ideal partner.

**Part 2:**
**Expectations and Promises**

: This part details what the writer expects from her language exchange partner and what she offers in return. It sets the expectations for the exchange, emphasizing mutual learning and cultural exchange.

If you're interested in this language exchange opportunity, please reach out to me. We can start by chatting online and maybe even plan some video calls. I'm really excited about this and I hope to find someone who shares my enthusiasm for learning.

To contact me, please send an email to a_youngjj@kmail.com. Don't hesitate to introduce yourself and share a little bit about why you're interested in the language exchange. I'm looking forward to hearing from you!

Thank you for reading my post. I can't wait to embark on this language adventure with one of you!

**Conclusion**

: It is a call to action. The writer finishes by inviting readers to contact her if they are interested and expresses her excitement about the language exchange.

Comic made at Pixton.com

Comic made at Pixton.com

## What is a CTA in advertisements?

: **Call to Action (CTA)** is crucial in any advertisement, including blog posts. A CTA is a clear statement or instruction designed to encourage the reader to take a specific action, such as reaching out to initiate the language exchange.

## Why are they important?

• **Encourages Action**: A CTA clearly tells readers what they should do next. This helps turn readers into responders.

• **Boosts Engagement**: By including a CTA, students invite their readers to engage directly with them. This can lead to more responses and interactions, helping readers make connections with the writer.

• **Provides Direction**: A CTA helps guide their readers on how to respond, making the communication process smoother and more straightforward for both sides.

Comic made at Pixton.com

▪ **Keep it simple:** Use language that's easy to understand and avoid complex words or phrases.

▪ **Be enthusiastic:** Convey your excitement about the language exchange opportunity through your words.

▪ **Include instructions:** If they need to comment, email, or fill out a form, make sure to say so clearly.

▪ **Safety first:** Remind them to discuss with a parent or guardian before making contact.

## Examples of CTA

**e.g.,** Want to learn more together? Send me a message!

**e.g.,** Let's be language buddies! Contact me to start!

**e.g.,** Interested in a fun exchange? Reach out to me!

**e.g.,** Help me learn Spanish, and I'll help you with English! Message me!

**e.g.,** Ready to explore languages together? Let's chat!

## DEEP DIVE

**A.** Look at the model text. Then answer the questions.

1. What genre does the text belong to?

2. What is the purpose of the text?

3. How many parts are in the text? Can you explain the function of each part?


**B.** Look at the model text. Then answer the questions.

1. Who was the reader of the text?

2. Who was the writer?

3. How close is the reader and the writer? How do you know it?

4. Find one example that shows the relationship between the reader and the writer from the model text.


**C.** Fill in the blanks with the body parts. Read the text below and circle the writer and reader. Then underline the purpose of this text.


Hi everyone! I'm Sally, a 14-year-old student from Australia. Through this blog, I'm reaching out to find a special language exchange friend. I'm super excited about learning Korean while helping someone with their English!

I've always been fascinated by Korean culture and have recently started learning the language. But, I know the best way to improve is by actually speaking it. That's why I'm looking for a Korean girl around 14 to 15 years old who's interested in improving her English and can help me with my Korean speaking skills.

What I'm looking for in a language exchange partner:

A native Korean speaker who wants to get better at English.
Someone my age, so we have similar interests and experiences.
A friendly and patient partner, as we're both learning and growing.
What I offer as a language exchange partner:

Help with English speaking, from basic conversations to more complex ones.
A chance to learn about Australian culture, lifestyle, and traditions.
A supportive and understanding environment to practice and make mistakes.

I believe language exchange is a fantastic way to learn. It's not just about language; it's about cultural exchange, making a new international friend, and learning how to communicate in real-life situations. I'm really looking forward to practicing Korean in a fun, relaxed way.

If you're a Korean girl wanting to improve your English and are willing to help me with Korean, I'd love to hear from you! We can chat online, exchange messages, and maybe even have video calls. I'm very enthusiastic about this journey and can't wait to start.

To get in touch with me, please email me at sally_cute@kmail.com. You can tell me your name and why you want to learn together. I can't wait to hear from you.

Thank you for checking out my post. Let's embark on this exciting language-learning adventure together!

Comic made at Pixton.com

**TIP 1**                                       **TITLE**

The title should be like a friendly wave—it catches attention and invites people in.

| 7    Good example ✓ | Bad example X |
|---|---|
| Let's Swap Languages: Looking for an English-Speaking Friend!<br><br> Clear and inviting, specifies languages. | Hey!<br><br>Too vague, and doesn't explain the purpose of the post. |
| Join Me on a Language Learning Adventure!<br><br> Engaging and suggests a fun, shared activity. | I need to learn English now!<br><br> Sounds demanding and lacks politeness. |
| Seeking a Buddy to Learn English and Share Korean Culture!<br><br>Specifies the exchange and offers cultural sharing, making it appealing. | Whatever, just want a friend.<br><br> Sounds disinterested and lacks specificity. |

**EXERCISE 1.** Write appropriate titles for each scenario. Follow the example.

**e.g.,** You're a middle school student in the USA learning Spanish and you want to find a pen pal who speaks Spanish and wants to learn English. You're excited to exchange emails or letters, talking about your daily lives, hobbies, and maybe even share some jokes.

→ Hi! I'm Ethan, a 14-year-old from the USA who loves adventure, video games, and learning new things. I'm on a journey to learn Spanish and searching for a Spanish-speaking friend who wants to practice English. Let's talk about our hobbies, daily life, and maybe exchange some jokes. Can't wait to start this language adventure with you!"

**Situation 1.** You're passionate about music and are learning French. You want to find someone who speaks French and is interested in learning English, with the idea of sharing and discussing your favorite English and French songs as a way to learn together.

→
_____

**Situation 2.** As an aspiring artist who loves drawing, you're learning Japanese and would love to find a Japanese-speaking friend who wants to learn English. You hope to exchange drawings, discuss art, and share about your cultures through the language exchange.

→
_____

**Situation 3.** You have a passion for cooking and are fascinated by Italian cuisine. As someone learning Italian, you'd like to find a friend who speaks Italian and is interested in learning English. Your goal is to exchange recipes, cooking tips, and perhaps even cook together via video calls, exploring each other's cultures through the universal language of food.

→
_____

## HOW TO INTRODUCTION

Start with a warm greeting. Introduce yourself briefly, mentioning your name, age, country, and interests. State your goal of finding a language exchange partner to practice the aimed language while offering help with your language.

e.g., Hello! I'm Soo-min, a 13-year-old student from South Korea. I love K-pop, watching movies, and playing badminton. Currently, I'm learning English and I'm on the lookout for a friend who speaks English and wants to learn Korean. I'm excited to share about my culture and learn about yours. Let's embark on this language-learning journey together.

**EXERCISE 2.** Read the scenario above. Write an appropriate introduction for each scenario. Follow the example.

e.g., You're a middle school student in the USA learning Spanish and you want to find a pen pal who speaks Spanish and wants to learn English. You're excited to exchange emails or letters, talk about your daily lives, and hobbies, and maybe even share some jokes.

→ Hi! I'm Ethan, a 14-year-old from the USA who loves adventure, video games, and learning new things. I'm on a journey to learn Spanish and searching for a Spanish-speaking friend who wants to practice English. Let's talk about our hobbies, and daily life, and maybe exchange some jokes. Can't wait to start this language adventure with you!"

**Situation 1.**

→ _____

_____

**Situation 2.**

→ _____

_____

**Situation 3.**

→ _____

_____

Describe the kind of friend you're looking for, not just in language skills but also in any specific interests.   Mention the age range that might help you connect better.

**e.g.,** I hope to find a friend who is interested in learning Korean and can help me with my English. It would be great if you also enjoy K-pop or movies, but I'm eager to learn about your hobbies too! Age-wise, someone around 13-15 would be perfect so we have more in common.

Explain what you can offer to your language exchange partner. This could include teaching Korean, sharing cultural insights, and discussing shared interests.

**e.g.,** I can teach you Korean, from basic phrases to more advanced expressions, especially if you like K-pop lyrics! We can also talk about Korean movies and I can share some cool cultural facts. Plus, I'm ready to learn about your interests and share language tips.

**EXERCISE 3.** Read the scenario above. Write an appropriate looking for and offering for each scenario. Follow the example.

**e.g.,** You're a middle school student in the USA learning Spanish and you want to find a pen pal who speaks Spanish and wants to learn English. You're excited to exchange emails or letters, talk about your daily lives, and hobbies, and maybe even share some jokes.

**Looking for:**
I want to find a friend who is my age and speaks Spanish. I hope you like video games and adventures too, but if not, that's okay! I'm excited to learn about what you like."

**Offering:**
I can help you with your English, especially with writing and reading. We can talk about your favorite hobbies and I can share about life in the USA. I also know some really good jokes to make you laugh!"

**Situation 1.**

**Look for:** _____

_____

_____

**Offering:** _____

_____

_____

**Situation 2.**

**Look for:** _____

_____

_____

**Offering:** _____

_____

_____

**Situation 3.**

**Look for:** _____

_____

_____

**Offering:** _____

_____

_____

**TIP4**                                   REASONS

Share your reasons for wanting a language exchange. Highlight the benefits of learning languages together and exchanging cultural insights.

e.g., I believe learning languages is more fun and effective when we do it together. We can correct each other's mistakes, learn slang and expressions that aren't in textbooks, and get a glimpse of each other's world. It's like having a friend to guide you through the language-learning maze!

**EXERCISE 4.** Read the scenario above. Write an appropriate reason for each scenario. Follow the example.

e.g., You're a middle school student learning Spanish and you want to find a pen pal who speaks Spanish and wants to learn English. You're excited to exchange emails or letters, talk about your daily lives, and hobbies, and maybe even share some jokes.

→ Learning with a friend is more fun than learning alone. We can help each other with new words and practice speaking. It's a great way to learn about different cultures and make a new friend.

**Situation 1.**

→
_____

_____

_____

**Situation 2.**

→
_____

_____

_____

**Situation 3.**

→
_____

_____

_____

**CONCLUSION:**

Close your post with a friendly invitation for readers to contact you if they're interested. Express your excitement about starting this journey.

**e.g.,** If you're interested in becoming language buddies and exploring each other's cultures, please send me an email. I'm looking forward to making a new friend and improving our language skills together. Thank you for reading my post, and let's start our fun and exciting language exchange!

**EXERCISE 5.** Read the scenario above. Write an appropriate conclusion for each scenario. Follow the example.

**e.g.,** You're a middle school student learning Spanish and you want to find a pen pal who speaks Spanish and wants to learn English. You're excited to exchange emails or letters, talk about your daily lives, and hobbies, and maybe even share some jokes.

→ If you're interested in exchanging letters or emails and learning together, please write to me. I'm looking forward to sharing stories and learning Spanish with you. Thank you for reading my post. Let's begin our adventure in languages together!

**Situation 1.**

→ _____

_____

_____

**Situation 2.**

→ _____

_____

_____

**Situation 3.**

→ _____

_____

_____

- **Be Yourself**

: Your post is a way to show your personality. Write like you speak to sound more natural and friendly.

- **Be Clear and Simple**

: Use simple language and short sentences to make your post easy to understand for everyone.

- **Be Kind and Respectful**

: Always use polite words and show respect for the people reading your post. Making friends starts with kindness.

## DEEP DIVE

**A.** Read the letter below. Compare it with the Model Text. Discuss with your partner about the given text.

**Title:** I need to learn English now!

My name's Lee. You must be a native English speaker, no exceptions. You can learn Korean from me but don't expect too much. That's it. Bye.

**B.** Read the Model Text. Underline **Tip1–6** in the text.

**SUMMARY**                                    **BLOG POSTING**

Process of Writing a Blog Post: (1) **Start with a Catchy Title**. It should grab
attention. (2) **Begin with a Friendly Introduction**. (3) **State Your Purpose in the
Opening Paragraphs.** Clearly explain why you're writing the post. (4) **Provide More
Information.** Go into more detail. (5) **End with a Call to Action and a Polite
Closing**. Encourage readers to respond if they're interested. Include any preferred
contact details or how they can get in touch with you through the blog. Finish with a
friendly sign-off.

**Title**            {

**Introduction**     { *Hello,*


                     { *Main purpose*
                                                                    }
                                                                    }  **Main body**
                     { *More information*                           }


**Reason**           {


**Conclusion**       { *Call to Action*

**A Few Days Later**

Comic made at Pixton.com

**I am eager to** immerse myself in the English language by reading lots of books.

**I am eager to** take every opportunity to learn new things.

People say *I am eager to* when they want to express that they are very excited and looking forward to doing something. It's like when you can't wait for something fun to happen, like a birthday party or going on a field trip. When you use *I am eager to*, you're telling someone that you're really happy and excited about what's going to happen next.

After *I am eager to* always use the verb in its base form. No "ing" or "ed" endings right after *I am eager to*.

e.g., *I am eager to* share my enthusiasm for science with my classmates.

e.g., *I am eager to* reach out to new friends in my class.

**EXERCISE 7.** Read the given situations. Write your own sentences with *I am eager to...* Follow the example.

| Situation | |
|---|---|
| **e.g.,** You are very excited about your vacation. | e.g., I am eager to go on vacation. |
| 1. You can't wait to find out more about dinosaurs because you think they're interesting. | → |
| 2. You are really looking forward to being part of the team and playing soccer. | → |
| 3. You are very excited and looking forward to meeting new people and forming friendships with them. | → |

**EXERCISE 8.** Read the situations and write your own sentences to complete them. Follow the example.

**e.g.,** You are excited about discovering what the museum has to show.
What will you say?

→ *I am eager to* explore the city museum during our field trip.

1. You want to express your enthusiasm to practice and enhance your drawing abilities.
What will you say?

→_____

2. You want to show your enthusiasm about beginning a new musical journey by learning to play an instrument.
What will you say?

→_____

3. You want to show your excitement about being involved in the science fair.
What will you say?

→_____

**EXERCISE 9.** Write your own sentences using *I am eager to...*

1._____

2._____

3._____

4._____

# DEEP DIVE

**A.** Read the Model Text again. Why did the writer say *I am eager to...*? Discuss with your partner.

## A COLON AND INTRODUCING DETAILS

Comic made at Pixton.com

The colon is a punctuation mark used to indicate that what follows it is an explanation, a list, or a quotation related to what precedes it.

### Why Use a Colon (:)?

A colon (:) is used to introduce something more specific related to what was mentioned before it.

**1. To introduce a list**: A colon can introduce a list of items.
**e.g.,** For our picnic, we need to bring several things.
**e.g.,** For our picnic, we need to bring several things: sandwiches, lemonade, cookies, and a blanket.

**2. To introduce a quote:** A colon can be used before a quote.
**e.g.,** My favorite author once said something important.
**e.g.,** My favorite author once said something important: 'Reading is a journey into new worlds.'

**3. To introduce an explanation or example:** A colon can be used to explain something further or provide an example.
**e.g.,** There's one hobby I enjoy more than others.
**e.g.,** There's one hobby I enjoy more than others: reading.

### How to Use a Colon?

1. Make sure the part **before the colon can stand as a complete sentence.**

2. The information **after the colon provides more detail about what was mentioned before it.**

EXERCISE 11. Read the sentence. Add a colon in each sentence. Follow the examples.

| Introducing a List | |
| --- | --- |
| **Without a colon** | **With a colon** |
| e.g., We need a few volunteers for the school event. | e.g., We need a few volunteers for the school event: two for registration, one for setup, and another for cleanup. |
| e.g., She has visited many countries. | |
| e.g., To make a smoothie, you need some ingredients. | |
| **Introducing a Quote** | |
| **Without a colon** | **With a colon** |
| e.g., The scientist made a significant observation. | e.g., The scientist made a significant observation: 'The smallest particles can have the biggest impact on our theories.' |
| e.g., The coach gave us advice before the game. | |
| e.g., Our principal started the assembly with a powerful message. | |
| **Introducing an Explanation or Example** | |
| **Without a colon** | **With a colon** |
| e.g., He has a clear favorite genre of music. | e.g., He has a clear favorite genre of music: jazz |
| e.g., There's a reason she always feels at peace in the garden. | |
| e.g., Our teacher emphasized a critical aspect of learning. | |

EXERCISE 12. Read the Model text. Find a colon and underline. Think why the writer uses a colon. Work with your partner.

## DEEP DIVE

A.   When we see a colon in the sentence, is it possible to guess the function of it at a glance? Discuss with your partner.

# MORE EXERCISE FOR GRAMMAR1

**Exercise 1.** Read the sentence. Add a colon in each sentence.

To complete the project, you'll need a notebook along with colored pencils, glue, and scissors.

→ _____

The possible responses to the question include yes, no, maybe, and I don't know.

→ _____

I can assure you of three things which are honesty, hard work, and dedication.

→ _____

The assignment requires you to bring a map of your state, a list of state symbols, and a short history.

→ _____

Before we see off the guest speaker, let's prepare a thank you card, a bouquet of flowers, and a small gift.

→ _____

Our coach would assure us by saying 'Victory is in the effort, not just the outcome.'

→ _____

The professor stated 'Every assignment is a step towards your future.'

→ _____

A key to a successful assignment is understanding the instructions by knowing exactly what is asked.

→ _____

When you make a request, be polite, specific, and express gratitude.

→ _____

Comic made at Pixton.com

**Two Main Uses**

**1. Time:** When we use *as* to talk about time, it means two actions are happening simultaneously.
**e.g., *As* I eat, I read. = I am eating and reading** *at the same time.*

**2. Reason:** When we use *as* to talk about a reason, it explains why something is happening.
**e.g., *As* it's raining, I will take an umbrella. = I'm taking an umbrella** *because* **it is raining.**

Remember these two rules.

1. *As* and a Full Sentence:
e.g., As I open my book (first full sentence), I find my favorite story (second full sentence).

2. Using a Comma:
e.g., *As* I tie my shoes (comma →), I get ready to go out.

40

**EXERCISE 17.** Read the sentences in the chart below. Figure out the function of as in the sentences. Follow the example.

| Sentence | Time | Reason | Sentence | Time | Reason |
|---|---|---|---|---|---|
| As the sun rises, the birds start to sing. | √ | | As I was late, I missed the beginning of the meeting. | | |
| As the road was closed, we took a different route. | | | As we watched the movie, we ate popcorn. | | |
| As the water boiled, he prepared the tea leaves. | | | As the snow fell, children built snowmen outside. | | |
| s it was getting dark, we turned on the lights. | | | As the weather was nice, we went for a picnic. | | |
| As the music played, they danced together. | | | As the library was quiet, it was the perfect place to study. | | |

**EXERCISE 18.** Read the parts of the sentences below. Match them with the correct part.

As I wake up,               •          •      we talk about our favorite games.

As we walk to school,       •          •      the dog runs around them.

As it's hot outside,        •          •      I'm studying tonight.

As the library is closed,   •          •      she listens to music.

As we have a test tomorrow, •          •      I'm drinking lots of water.

As they play outside,       •          •      I'll go to bed early.

As I'm feeling tired,       •          •      I'll read at home.

As she does her homework,   •          •      I stretch my arms.

**EXERCISE 19.** Read the given sentences. Find mistakes and correct them.

1. As I reach out to make new friends I feel a little nervous but excited.

2. As I see an opportunity to join the soccer team, quickly sign up.

3. As we exchange stickers I find one I've been looking for a long time.

4. As look for my lost pencil, clean my messy desk.

5. As wait patiently for my turn, I read a book to pass the time.

# MORE EXERCISE FOR GRAMMAR2

**EXERCISE 1.** Read the sentences in the chart below. Figure out the function of as in the sentences. Follow the example.

| Sentence | Time | Reason | Sentence | Time | Reason |
|---|---|---|---|---|---|
| As I study, I listen to music. | | | As it's raining, we'll play indoors today. | | |
| As it's hot today, we're going to the pool. | | | As the dog saw the cat, it started to bark. | | |
| As it's the weekend, I can stay up late. | | | As she talks on the phone, she walks around the room. | | |

**EXERCISE 2.** Read the parts of the sentences below. Match them with the correct part.

As my enthusiasm for drawing grows,   •                    •   I forget about the time.

As I immerse myself in painting   •                    •   I find interesting club activities.

As I reach out to my friend in class   •                    •   I learn about my friend's favorite cartoon.

As we exchange stickers   •                    •   I feel less alone.

As I navigate the school website   •                    •   I fill up my sketchbook with new art.

**EXERCISE 3.** Read the given sentences. Find mistakes and correct them.

1. As my teacher gives us insight into the science project I take careful notes.

2. As move to more advanced math problems, ask my teacher for extra help.

3. As navigating the new video game, discovering hidden secrets.

4. As I immerse myself in learning Spanish I start to understand the songs.

## DEEP DIVE

**A.** When do people use *as* in sentences? Discuss with your partner.

**B.** What *as* is used in the Model text? What is the advantage of using *as* in the sentences? Discuss with your partner.

## HANDS-ON ACTIVITIES

**A.** Look at the picture. Write sentences using given words. Follow the example.

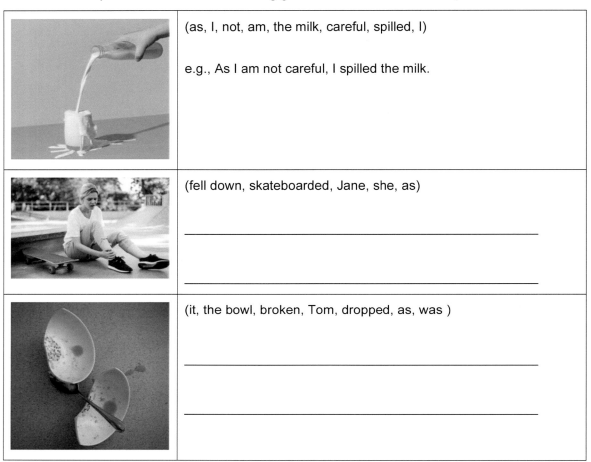

| | |
|---|---|
| | (as, I, not, am, the milk, careful, spilled, I)<br><br>e.g., As I am not careful, I spilled the milk. |
| | (fell down, skateboarded, Jane, she, as)<br><br>_____<br><br>_____ |
| | (it, the bowl, broken, Tom, dropped, as, was )<br><br>_____<br><br>_____ |

**B.** Write your own sentences with *as.* Work with your partner.

1._____

2._____

3._____

| [CLASS7] WRITE WITH YOUR TEACHER 1 | The purpose of this task is for you to practice blog posting. |
|---|---|

**You are writing a blog posting to look for a language exchange partner.**

**Write a blog that should include:**

• title,

• who you are,

• what you are looking for and can offer

• why you would like to exchange languages

• conclusion

• use *I am eager to* appropriately.

• use *as* appropriately.

## GAPS

| Genre: | | Purpose: | |
|---|---|---|---|
| Audience: | | Style: | |

## WRITE

| | |
|---|---|
| _____ <br><br> _____ <br><br><br> _____ <br><br><br><br> _____ <br><br> _____ | Title: _____ <br><br> _____. I really like Japanese culture and want to learn Japanese. I'm searching for a friend from Japan who wants to learn Korean. We can help each other! <br><br> Who I Am: <br> I'm just starting to learn Japanese and need some help. I know a lot about Korea and can help you learn Korean. I'm very excited to learn and help you too. <br><br> What I Need and What I Can Do: <br> I'm _____ a _____ friend because I'm still learning Japanese. I'll be _____ with you as you learn Korean. We can help each other get better. <br><br> Why I Want to Do This: <br> Learning with a friend is a great chance to know more than just language. <br> _____ <br><br> _____ <br><br> Let's learn and have fun together! _____ if you want to be friends and learn languages! _____ start and hope to talk to you soon. |

| CHECKLIST |
|---|
| • Did I use the appropriate title? _____ |
| • Did I use the appropriate blog posting structure? _____ |
| • Did I introduce and explain what I would like to do appropriately? _____ |
| • Did I use **as**? _____ |
| • Did I use *I am eager to* appropriately? _____ |
| • Did I understand the procedures of pre-writing, drafting, revising, and editing? _____ |

| **WRITE WITH YOUR TEACHER 2** | The purpose of this task is for you to practice blog posting. |
|---|---|

**You are writing a blog posting to look for a language exchange partner.**

**Write a blog that should include:**

• title,

• who you are,

• what you are looking for and can offer

• why you would like to exchange languages

• conclusion

• use *I am eager to* appropriately.

• use *as* appropriately.

## GAPS

| Genre: | | Audience: | |
|---|---|---|---|
| Purpose: | | Style: | |

## PREWRITING

## DRAFT

## FINAL DRAFT



## CHECKLIST

- Did I use the appropriate title? _____
- Did I use the appropriate blog posting structure? _____
- Did I introduce and explain what I would like to do appropriately? _____
- Did I use **as**? _____
- Did I use *I am eager to* appropriately? _____
- Did I understand the procedures of pre-writing, drafting, revising, and editing? _____

**Formative Assessment: HOMEWORK**

| HOMEWORK DAY 1 | KEYWORDS |
|---|---|

**1. Fill in the blanks with the words in the box below. You might need to change the form of the words (*e.g., play > playing, plays, or played*). The words might be used more than once or they might not be used at all.**

> reach out, opportunity, exchange, look for, patient, insight, advanced, navigate, immerse, enthusiasm

Title: Looking for a Chinese Language _____ Partner!

Hello everyone! I am Eun-chae, a Korean middle school student. I am on an exciting journey to learn Chinese. I am _____ through this blog to _____ a language _____ partner who is interested in learning Korean.

What I Am Looking For and Can Offer:

I am in search of someone who is _____ and has a good understanding of Chinese. It doesn't matter if you are not _____. We can learn and grow together. In return, I can help you with Korean. _____ share my knowledge and also learn from you.

Why I Want to Exchange Languages:

I believe that exchanging languages is a fantastic _____ to _____ ourselves in each other's cultures. It helps us to _____ through the learning process more smoothly. _____ gain insights into Chinese culture and language, which I think will make my journey more enjoyable and effective. My _____ for learning Chinese is as strong as my desire to help you learn Korean.

### Conclusion:

Let's embark on this language learning adventure together! I am looking forward to using this _____ as a way to enhance our understanding and abilities in our respective languages. If you're interested in this _____, please don't hesitate to _____ to me. Together, we can create a supportive and enriching learning environment.

Thank you for reading my blog post. _____ hear from you soon!

**1. Fill in the blanks with the words in the box below. You might need to change the form of the words (*e.g., play > playing, plays, or played*). The words might be used more than once or they might not be used at all.**

> reach out, opportunity, exchange, look for, patient, insight, advanced, navigate, immerse, enthusiasm

Title: _____ a Spanish Exchange Partner for My Spain Adventure!

Hello everyone. My name is Alex, and I am a 15-year-old middle school student. I am _____ a Spanish language _____ partner. I want to prepare for my upcoming trip to Spain!

_____ learn Spanish because I believe it will help me _____ the country better and _____ myself in its beautiful culture. In return, I can offer help with Korean. I have a lot of _____ for learning and teaching!

Why do I want to _____ languages? Well, I think it's a fantastic _____ to gain _____ into another culture and make new friends. Plus, it will be super helpful for my trip. I am _____ and ready to learn as well as teach.

In conclusion, if you are looking to improve your Korean and are _____ enough to teach a beginner Spanish, please _____ to me. This could be a great chance for both of us to advance in our language-learning journey!

Thank you for considering my request. I can't wait to start this exciting _____ with you!

**2. Read again and find the GAPS of the given text above. Then complete the table below.**

| Genre: | Audience: |
|---|---|
| Purpose: | Style: |

**3. Write about the structure of the blog posting.**

**4. Write about the CTA.**

1. Fill in the blanks with the words in the box below. You might need to change the form of the words (*e.g., play > playing, plays, or played*). The words might be used more than once or they might not be used at all.

> reach out, opportunity, exchange, look for, patient, insight, advanced, navigate, immerse, enthusiasm

Title: _____ a French-English Language _____ Buddy!

Hello! My name is Alex, and I am a middle school student. I love learning new languages. I am _____ someone who wants to _____ languages. I can help you with English, and I would like to learn French.

I want to _____ languages because I plan to travel to Europe soon. Learning French will help me _____ new places and _____ myself in different cultures. I believe that speaking a little bit of the local language makes traveling more fun and meaningful.

I am eager to meet someone who is _____ and willing to teach me French. In return, I promise to share my knowledge of English. This is a great _____ for us to learn from each other and gain new _____ into our languages and cultures.

I am very enthusiastic about this language _____. If you are interested in learning English and can help me with French, please _____ to me. Let's take this chance to improve our language skills together!

This experience will not only help me prepare for my trip to Europe but also allow us to make new friends. Let's learn and grow together with patience and _____!

2. Write about 6 and additional tips for writing a blog posting

**1. Fill in the blanks with the words in the box below. You might need to change the form of the words (*e.g., play > playing, plays, or played*). The words might be used more than once or they might not be used at all.**

> reach out, opportunity, exchange, look for, patient, insight, advanced, navigate, immerse, enthusiasm, I am eager to

_____ a Korean Language Buddy!

Hi! I'm Rosa, a middle school student looking for a Korean language _____ partner. _____ learn Korean because I'm planning to visit Korea.

What I Offer and Seek:
I can help with English, and I hope to find someone _____ and excited about sharing Korean language and culture.

Why Exchange?
_____ languages is a great way to learn and understand each other's culture. I want to _____ myself in Korean culture and _____ my way around Korea with ease.

If you want to improve your English and can help me with Korean, please _____!
Let's make learning fun and prepare for our adventures with _____.

Looking forward to hearing from you!

**2. When can we use *I am eager to*? Give one example that the expression can be used.**

52

**3. Read the situation use *please let me know* to complete sentences.**

**Situation 1**: You want to borrow 'Harry Potter' from the school library but are not sure if it's available. You ask the librarian.

_____.

**Situation 2:** You want to join the school's art club but don't know when they meet. You ask a club member.

_____.

**Situation 3**: You want to know if the science project is a group assignment. You ask your science teacher by email.

_____.

**Situation 4:** You want to find out what you need to bring for the class picnic. You ask your teacher.

_____.

**Situation 5:** You want to know if there is homework in math class as you were absent yesterday. You ask your classmate.

_____.

**1. Fill in the blanks with the words in the box below. You might need to change the form of the words (*e.g., play > playing, plays, or played*). The words might be used more than once or they might not be used at all.**

> reach out, opportunity, exchange, look for, patient, insight, advanced, navigate, immerse, enthusiasm, I am eager to, :

Seeking a Chinese-Korean Language Exchange Partner!

Hello there! My name is Yu, a middle school student from China. I'm _____ through this blog to look for a Korean language _____ partner. _____ find someone who is _____ and willing to help me improve my Korean speaking skills. In return, I can offer my assistance in learning Chinese, whether you're a beginner or looking to advance your skills.

I believe that language _____ is a fantastic _____ to not only learn a new language but also to gain _____ into another culture. My main goal is to _____ the challenges of learning Korean and _____ myself fully in the language to prepare for an upcoming speaking test. As someone who loves languages, I bring a lot of _____ to the table and _____ always _____learn and share.

Why am I seeking this _____, you might ask? _____
I've always been fascinated by Korean culture and language. By partnering with a Korean speaker who wants to learn Chinese, we can help each other reach our language learning goals. It's a great way to practice speaking and listening in a real-world context, and I'm sure we can both benefit from the _____ and experiences we share.

If you're interested in a language _____ and think we could help each other out, please don't hesitate to _____. _____start this language learning journey and make the most of this _____. Let's _____ this exciting adventure together with patience, _____, and a genuine love for learning!

Looking forward to hearing from you soon!

**2. Write about the function of *a colon*.**

**3. Read the sentences. Change the sentences using a colon. Follow the examples.**

**e.g.,** We need to buy a lot of fruits for the party, such as apples, bananas, oranges, and grapes.
→ We need to buy a lot of fruits for the party: apples, bananas, oranges, and grapes.

1. The rules of the game are simple you must not touch the ball with your hands, play fair, and respect the referee.
→

2. To become a better reader, you should follow these steps read every day, explore various genres, and discuss what you read with others.
→

3. The ingredients for the cake include eggs, flour, sugar, and butter.".
→

4. "He mentioned his favorite sports which are soccer, basketball, and tennis."
→

5. For the science project, you will need several items including a poster board, markers, glue, and scissors.
→

**1. Fill in the blanks with the words in the box below. You might need to change the form of the words (*e.g., play > playing, plays, or played*). The words might be used more than once or they might not be used at all.**

> reach out, opportunity, exchange, look for, patient, insight, advanced, navigate, immerse, enthusiasm, I am eager to, :, as

Title: Want to Watch Anime Together? Let's Learn Languages!

Hi! I'm Hye-yen, a middle school student from Korea. I love Japanese anime and want to find a friend who can help me learn Japanese. I'm also happy to help you with Korean.

What I Offer and Seek_____
I'm looking for a language _____ partner who loves anime as much as I do. _____to learn and _____, and I hope you are too. Together, we can enjoy anime and improve our language skills!

Why?
I want to understand anime better by learning Japanese and share my love for Korean culture with you. It's a great _____ for both of us to learn something new and make a new friend.

If you're interested in watching anime and learning together, please _____. Let's start this fun journey filled with anime and languages!

Hope to hear from you soon!

**2. Write about how *as* works in the sentences.**

**3. Read the text. Underline time as and circle reason as.**

As Max woke up, he could hear the birds singing. It was a bright Saturday morning. As it was sunny, Max decided to go to the park. He called his friend Lily and asked if she wanted to join. "As I have no plans today, I'd love to come," Lily replied.

As they walked to the park, they talked about their favorite video games and movies. The park was not far, so as they arrived, they saw many people flying kites. "As it's windy, it's perfect weather for flying kites," Max said. They decided to watch the kites for a while.

After some time, they felt hungry. "As we're both hungry, let's eat something," suggested Lily. They found a small café nearby. As they ate their sandwiches, they planned their next adventure.

Suddenly, it started to rain. As it was raining, they decided to wait in the café until it stopped. "As we wait, we can play cards," Lily said, pulling out a deck from her bag. They played several rounds of cards, laughing and enjoying their time.

The rain stopped and the sun came back out, drying the wet streets. "As the sun is out again, we can go back to the park," Max suggested. They spent the rest of the afternoon there, enjoying the fresh air and making plans for their next meeting.

**1. Fill in the blanks with the words in the box below. You might need to change the form of the words (*e.g., play > playing, plays, or played*). The words might be used more than once or they might not be used at all.**

> reach out, opportunity, exchange, look for, patient, insight, advanced, navigate, immerse, enthusiasm, I am eager to, :, as

Seeking Korean-Spanish Language Exchange Partner for K-Dramas!

Hi everyone! I'm María, a middle school student. _____ learn Korean through K-Dramas. I'm _____ a _____ language _____ partner to learn together.

I can offer _____ into Spanish while I learn Korean. Let's advance our language skills together! I'm excited about _____ languages to explore new cultures.

_____ a student, I have time in the evenings and weekends for language exchange. _____ if you're interested in joining me!

Thanks for considering this _____. _____ connect and start learning!

| HOMEWORK DAY 7 | PRACTICE FOR YOUR INDEPENDENT WRITING |
|---|---|

**2.** You are a Korean middle school student and now you are writing a blog posting in English to look for a Korean-English language exchange partner for listening to pop songs.

Write a blog that should include

• title,

• who you are,

• what you are looking for and can offer

• why you would like to exchange languages

• conclusion

• use *I am eager to* appropriately.

• use *as* appropriately.

## GAPS

| Genre | | Audience | |
|---|---|---|---|
| Purpose | | Style | |

## PREWRITING

## DRAFT

## FINAL DRAFT

## CHECKLIST FOR REVISING AND EDITING

- Did I use the appropriate title? _____
- Did I use the appropriate blog posting structure? _____
- Did I introduce and explain what I would like to do appropriately? _____
- Did I use **as**? _____
- Did I use *I am eager to* appropriately? _____
- Did I understand the procedures of pre-writing, drafting, revising, and editing? _____

## Summative Assessment: Writing Portfolio Assignment (WPA)

| **INDEPENDENT WRITING** | The purpose of this task is for you to practice blog posting. |
|---|---|

You are an English middle school student and now you are writing a blog posting in English to look for a Korean-English language exchange partner for listening to K-pop songs.

Write a blog that should include

• title,

• who you are,

• what you are looking for and can offer

• why you would like to exchange languages

• conclusion

• use *I am eager to* appropriately.

• use *as* appropriately.

### GAPS

| Genre: | | Audience: | |
|---|---|---|---|
| Purpose: | | Style: | |

### PREWRITING

### DRAFT

## FINAL DRAFT









## CHECKLIST FOR REVISING AND EDITING

• Did I use the appropriate title? _____

• Did I use the appropriate blog posting structure? _____

• Did I introduce and explain what I would like to do appropriately? _____

• Did I use **as**? _____

• Did I use *I am eager to* appropriately? _____

• Did I understand the procedures of pre-writing, drafting, revising, and editing? _____

# BLOG POSTING RUBRIC FOR MODULE 9

| BAND | GENRE FEATURES | COHERENCE AND COHESION | LEXICAL RESOURCE | GRAMMATICAL RANGE AND ACCURACY OF AS, AND A COLON | TASK ACHIEVEMENT |
|---|---|---|---|---|---|
| 3 | Correctly uses the typical structure of a blog posting. Includes an appropriate title and details with politeness. | Well-organized, with clear connections between sentences, and uses reasoning to help readers better understand. | Utilizes a simple range of vocabulary correctly and effectively, suitable for A1 level. | Uses basic grammatical structures, and punctuation, especially *as*, *colons, and I am eager to* accurately and effectively, with no or very few errors. | Fully completes the task by appropriately addressing all aspects of the blog posting writing prompt with simple yet accurate supporting ideas. |
| 2 | Partially includes blog posting genre features with polite sentences, but some key elements may be missing or inadequately executed. | Generally well-organized but may lack some coherence in sentence connections or reasoning. | Uses some suitable vocabulary but may lack variety or contain some words not used correctly. | Uses grammatical structures, and punctuation, especially *as*, *colons, and I am eager to* but may contain errors that sometimes obstruct understanding. | Partially completes the task by addressing some aspects of the prompt with a few relevant but simple supporting ideas; however, some aspects might be lacking. |
| 1 | Largely misses a blog posting genre features, and includes inappropriate elements for an instruction. | Disorganized or lacks logical flow from one sentence to another. | Shows a lack of vocabulary variety or contains many words used incorrectly. | Lacks accuracy in the use of punctuation, *as*, *colons, and I am eager to* make the text difficult to understand. | Largely fails to address the blog posting writing prompt appropriately or lacks the necessary supporting ideas. |
| 0 | The blog posting is not written | | | | |

## Formative Evaluation: Teachers' diaries and records

| Name of student (grade in school) | | |
|---|---|---|
| Date | Diary | Record |
| | | |
| | | |

**Summative Evaluation: Student Survey Questionnaire**

| Rating scale questions | | 1 = "strongly disagree"<br>5 = "strongly agree" | | | | |
|---|---|---|---|---|---|---|
| **1** | The goals of the course were clear and appropriate. | 1 | 2 | 3 | 4 | 5 |
| **2** | I was clearly stated my responsibilities and course requirements at the beginning. | 1 | 2 | 3 | 4 | 5 |
| **3** | The assessment used in the course was appropriate and fair. | 1 | 2 | 3 | 4 | 5 |
| **4** | The materials used in the course were appropriate and useful. | 1 | 2 | 3 | 4 | 5 |
| **5** | The texts and topics covered were interesting and relevant. | 1 | 2 | 3 | 4 | 5 |
| **6** | I was given clear instructions and explained things well. | 1 | 2 | 3 | 4 | 5 |
| **7** | I was given enough chances to write. | 1 | 2 | 3 | 4 | 5 |
| **8** | The lessons contained an appropriate variety of activities. | 1 | 2 | 3 | 4 | 5 |
| **Open-ended questions** | | | | | | |
| **9** | What did you like most about the course? | | | | | |
| **10** | What did you like least about the course? | | | | | |

# Guided by Growth

**1** This section provides a concise introduction to the key concepts and interrelations of TCL, genre writing, and process writing, which form the foundational methodology of this book. A thoughtful and thorough reading of this section is essential, as it will significantly benefit your understanding and participation in the class/

**2** This document is a guide that provides a sample lesson plan to help teachers in their teaching process. Teachers don't have to follow it exactly, and it can be adjusted based on the teacher's experience and the needs of the students.

Using this guide could be very helpful for new teachers or those not very experienced with making lesson plans. It allows teachers to make their own lesson plans suitable for their students and their teaching situation.

This guide supports a detailed and effective way of planning lessons, making teachers more flexible and creative in their teaching strategies. This way, teaching becomes more focused on the students' needs, helping them learn in a way that's best for them.

**3** Often, due to tight class schedules, instructors rush into lessons without clarifying the objectives. This lack of context is a key reason why students might not find the class engaging. By discussing questions and exchanging views with students, educators can leverage their existing knowledge and spark curiosity in the subject matter.

While many Korean English learners might not naturally choose to write diaries in English, I've included a diary module in this book for several reasons. Firstly, it's an excellent way to practice past tenses and improve coherence and cohesion. Many learners find it challenging to freely express their personal experiences and feelings in English, and the diary format can help break down these barriers. Plus, this module offers a chance to explore different ways of expressing time, rather than sticking to just one approach.

**4** Learning keywords is a gradual process, not something that occurs instantly. A learner needs multiple exposures to a word to learn it effectively. The texts within a module generally reuse many of the words, facilitating this repetitive exposure. Additionally, there are more extensive learning resources available in the assignments towards the end of the book, which can be highly beneficial, so be sure to make good use of them. Most vocabulary learning focuses on linking words in Korean and English, but it's also crucial to remember the importance of learners consistently hearing the pronunciation and accent of essential words.

In this book, webtoons play a pivotal role in showcasing why this genre stands out uniquely. Instead of casually browsing through the webtoons, teachers should motivate learners by having them read in groups or participate in role-playing activities. Furthermore, guiding them through the webtoon dialogues will help them understand the essence of the genre and the book's overarching narrative

The term "call to action" itself might be unfamiliar to students. When it comes to blog postings, most Korean students might think of sharing their lives on Instagram or Facebook. However, starting from explaining various types of blogs such as product reviews on Naver Blog, reviews after visiting places, posts about adopting cats or dogs, and even blogs for finding language exchange partners in foreign countries, can broaden the students' perspectives and increase their interest. Showing blog posts written in Korean can also be an effective method.

Many students may not be interested in the format of blog posts simply because they are not familiar with the different types of blog posts. Especially in the case of their personal accounts, which are only seen by their friends, they likely write without considering format or etiquette. Highlighting these aspects is necessary to emphasize the purpose of the blog post we are writing. From there, we can piece together the larger picture, such as why it's important not to use overly casual language, why vague words should be avoided, how to attract the reader's interest and keep them engaged until the end, ways to provide convincing reasons, and how to properly conclude the post.

Here, what we call "Common Sayings" are also widely recognized as "fixed expressions." Learning these as whole patterns, instead of dissecting their grammatical structures, can be more beneficial for learners. Although expressions like "I am eager to" are frequently used, I have rarely seen students use them in everyday conversation or writing, despite memorizing them for exams. The expressions included in this book might mostly be ones that students are already familiar with. However, the purpose of this book is to encourage their use. I included them in the hope that students can practice and use these expressions more actively.

When looking at the writing of Korean students, the punctuation they use is mostly limited to commas, periods, double quotes, and single quotes. They are relatively less exposed to other common

punctuation marks used in various genres, such as colons, semicolons, hyphens, en dashes, and em dashes. As a result, although they are interested, they often misuse them due to lack of instruction. While not all punctuation marks will be covered in this series of books, I included the use of colons to show how they are used in English, hoping that students will learn how to use them correctly, especially since colons are also commonly used in Korean.

 **10**

If you look up "as" in an English dictionary, you will find that it has 17 different meanings. However, I thought that there are mainly two usages that the students need to know: time and reason. When expressions of time or reason are well used, the liveliness of the writing is enhanced and the logical flow of the text improves. Therefore, I wanted to emphasize these two aspects.

# [닫는 말]

**Discover Writing Discover Korea** 시리즈는 단순한 영어 학습서가 아닌, 한국 문화의 심장으로의 여행입니다. 이 시리즈 안에서 학습자들과 선생님들은 언어 학습과 문화적 몰입이 동시에 어우러진 독특한 경험을 할 수 있습니다. 일상 생활에서 먼 거리에 있던 그동안의 영어학습과 달리, 이 시리즈는 그 간극을 메워 교육적이면서도 공감 가능한 학습 경험을 제공합니다.

또한, 이 시리즈는 언어 학습에 새로운 시각을 제시합니다. 한국 문화, 관습 및 경험을 영어 교육에 엮음으로써 종합적인 접근 방식으로 언어를 습득할 기회를 제공합니다.

**저는 여기에서 멈추지 않고 이 시리즈를 확장하고 한국 문화, 역사 및 현대 생활의 풍부함을 더 깊이 탐구하고 다른 장르로 확장할 계획이며 영어 쓰기교육을 넘어 읽기, 듣기 및 말하기를 포함한 종합적인 자료를 만들고 싶습니다.**

흥미진진한 영어와 한국문화의 탐구 여정에 저와 함께 해보시면 어떨까요? 한 페이지 한 페이지마다 다양한 글의 장르와 한국을 탐험하면서 영어쓰기의 즐거움을 다시 발견해보세요. 독자가 되어 주심에 감사드리며, 앞으로의 만남을 기다리겠습니다.

2023 년 10 월 28 일

서은옥 드림

# [Epilogue]

The **Discover Writing Discover Korea** series is not just a set of English textbooks; it's a journey into the heart of Korean culture. In these pages, you'll find a unique blend of language learning and cultural immersion. These books bridge the gap that feels distant from our daily lives, making the learning experience not only educational but also relatable.

It offers a fresh perspective on language learning. By weaving Korean culture, customs, and experiences into English education, it provides a holistic approach to language acquisition.

**As for the future, my commitment is unwavering. I plan to expand this series, delving deeper into the richness of Korean culture, history, and modern life with other genres. I aim to create a comprehensive resource that not only enhances English writing skills but also reading listening and speaking, delving deeper into the richness of Korean culture, history, and modern life**.

So, join me in this exciting journey of language and culture. Rediscover the joy of learning as you explore different genres and Korea, one page at a time. Thank you for your support, and I look forward to sharing more with you in the future.

Sincerely,

Eun-ok Seo

# Discover Writing Discover Korea 9

**발 행** | 2024년 8월 5일

**저 자** | 서은옥

**펴낸이** | 한건희

**펴낸곳** | 주식회사 부크크

**출판사등록** | 2014.07.15(제2014-16호)

**주 소** | 서울특별시 금천구 가산디지털1로 119 SK트윈타워 A동 305호

**전 화** | 1670-8316

**이메일** | info@bookk.co.kr

**ISBN** | 979-11-410-9963-3

**www.bookk.co.kr**